CPS—MORRILL ELEMENTARY

34880004000787   629.4 WIL

Space

W9-BBN-005

DATE DUE

629.4   Williams, Brian.
WIL
          Space

          AR PTS: 2 RL: 7.7
CPS—MORRILL ELEMENTARY
   6011 S ROCKWELL ST
   CHICAGO, IL 60629

Space

Brian Williams

Heinemann Library
Chicago, Illinois

© 2002 Reed Educational and Professional Publishing
Published by Heinemann Library,
an imprint of Reed Educational & Professional Publishing,
Chicago, Illinois

Customer service 888-454-2279
Visit our website at www.heinemannlibrary.com.

All rights reserved. No part of this publication may be reproduced or transmitted in any form or by any means, electronic or mechanical, including photocopying, recording, taping, or any information storage and retrieval system, without permission in writing from the publisher.

Designed by Tinstar Design
Illustrations by Martin Griffin
Originated by Ambassador Litho
Printed by Wing King Tong in Hong Kong/China

06 05 04 03 02
10 9 8 7 6 5 4 3 2 1

Library of Congress Cataloging-in-Publication Data
Williams, Brian, 1959-
  Space / Brian Williams.
      p. cm. -- (Great inventions)
Includes bibliographical references and index.
  ISBN 1-58810-215-7
  1. Astronautics--Juvenile literature. 2. Outer
space--Exploration--Juvenile literature. [1. Astronautics. 2. Outer
space--Exploration.] I. Title. II. Series.
  TL793 .W553 2001
  629.4--dc21

                          2001000987

Acknowledgments
The author and publishers are grateful to the following for permission to reproduce copyright material:
Cover photographs: Corbis and Photodisc.
pp. 4, 22, 36, 40 Hulton; pp. 6, 19, 28 Science and Society Picture Library; pp. 8, 12 Science Photo Library; pp. 9, 14, 35, 37, 38, 41, 42 Corbis; pp. 10, 18, 23, 26, 30, 31, 32, 34 NASA/Science Photo Library; p. 13 Galia Jerrican/Science Photo Library; p. 16 Novosti; pp. 17, 24, 39 Genesis Space Photo; pp. 20, 21 Novosti/Science Photo Library; p. 29 NASA.

Every effort has been made to contact copyright holders of any material reproduced in this book. Any omissions will be rectified in subsequent printings if notice is given to the publisher.

Some words are shown in bold, **like this.** You can find out what they mean by looking in the glossary.

A note about dates: in this book, dates are followed by the letters B.C.E. (Before the Common Era) or C.E. (Common Era). This is instead of using the older abbreviations B.C. (Before Christ) and A.D. (*Anno Domini,* meaning "in the year of our Lord"). The date numbers are the same in both systems.

Contents

Introduction 4

Rocket, 1232 6

Telescope, 1608 8

Liquid-fueled Rocket, 1926 10

Radio Telescope, 1937....................................12

Satellite, 1957 14

Space Probe, 1959 16

Weather and Resources Satellites, 1960 18

Spy and Navigation Satellites, 1960 20

Manned Spacecraft, 1961 22

Space Suit, 1961 24

Moon Rocket, 1969 26

Moon Lander, 1969 28

Space Rover, 1970 30

Space Food and Fitness, 1971 32

Space Station, 1971 34

Mars Lander, 1976 36

Space Shuttle, 1981 38

Jet Pack, 1984 40

Space Telescope, 1990....................................42

Timeline...44

Glossary...46

More Books to Read 47

Index...48

Introduction

Space begins beyond the limits of Earth's atmosphere, the blanket of gases that wraps the planet in a warm, life-giving layer. Space is cold and airless. It begins above the height at which jet airplanes fly—6 to 7½ miles (10 to 12 kilometers)—and the highest point reached by balloons—about 25 miles (40 kilometers). To travel into space requires engines that do not need outside air to burn fuel, but can reach very high speeds to escape the pull of Earth's **gravity.** To survive in the emptiness of space, human explorers need to reproduce Earth's environment in the form of life-support systems that supply air, water, and food, and remove or recycle waste.

First dreams of space

People dreamed about traveling in space long before there were machines capable of taking them there. It was not until the 1500s that scientists understood how the planets moved in paths, or **orbits,** around the sun. In the early 1600s, they got their first closer look at the moon and the nearest planets through primitive telescopes.

Jules Verne and other science fiction writers created fantastic voyages through space and time in which ships could sail to the moon!

In 1865, the French writer Jules Verne wrote a science fiction story called *From the Earth to the Moon* in which people went to the Moon in a craft fired from a huge cannon. Space travel became one of the most popular subjects for science fiction writers. After the first airplane took to the skies in 1903, it seemed only a matter of time before real-life explorers matched the adventures of the fictional space fliers.

The inventions that made spaceflight happen

No single inventor made spaceflight happen. There are no Wright brothers, no Karl Benz, and no Thomas Edison in the history of space invention. Teams of scientists produced thousands of inventions to make the new technology work. Key inventions, such as telescopes and rockets, helped scientists learn more about the **solar system** and the many **galaxies** in the universe.

Spaceflight was impossible before 1900 because the technology needed to fly into space did not exist. In the early twentieth century, a handful of pioneers and amateurs exchanged ideas about the ways space might be explored. In the 1940s, military demands during World War II sped up work on new inventions, such as rockets, nuclear power, computers, and **radar.** In 1945, science writer Arthur C. Clarke suggested that space **satellites** might be used for worldwide radio and television communication.

Teamwork

By the 1950s, teams of scientists and engineers, most working in the United States and the **Soviet Union,** were building big rockets. In 1957, a rocket launched the first tiny satellite. The "space race" brought rapid advances in **electronics,** computers, medicine, and long-range communications.

The human space fliers or **astronauts** (called **cosmonauts** by the Russians) made headlines. The scientists and engineers who made everything from moon boots and space pens to giant rockets and robot planet-crawlers remained in the background. For every moon-walker on television, there were hundreds of people on the ground at mission control. Space exploration is a team effort and very expensive. This is why the latest space venture, the International Space Station, is a multinational project.

Rocket, 1232

Rockets were invented in China, probably soon after the invention of **gunpowder** some time before 1000 C.E., but their inventor is unknown. History books tell about how the Chinese used "arrows of flying fire" to fight off the Mongols in 1232 C.E. These were some of the first war rockets. Chinese inventors had made fireworks by filling paper or wooden tubes with gunpowder. Someone added a stick for balance, lit the bottom end, and when the tube flew into the air in a shower of sparks, the rocket was born.

The rocket's development

By the end of the 1200s, rockets were being used in battles across Asia and as far west as Spain. Inventors came up with crazy ideas for using rocket power. They dreamed up rocket-driven battering rams to knock down castle walls and rocket torpedoes to skim across the sea and wreck enemy ships. A Chinese legend tells about how, in about 1500, a man named Wan Hu tried to fly by tying 47 rockets and himself to two large kites. He disappeared in the explosion!

Congreve rockets made a lot of noise and smoke that added to their terrifying effect. Their "red glare" is mentioned in the words of the national anthem.

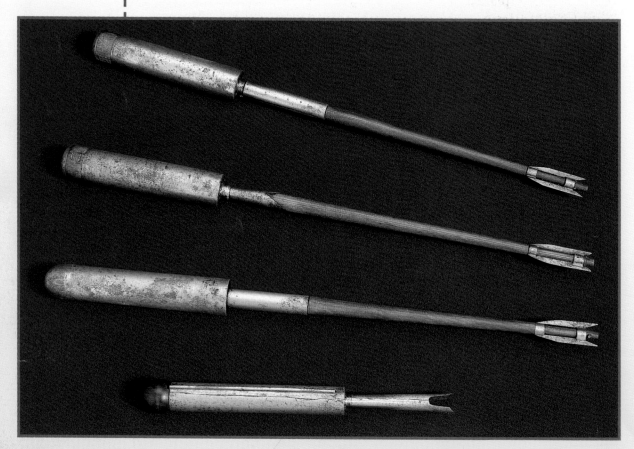

6

In the 1600s, a Polish inventor named Kazimierz Siemienowicz drew remarkable sketches of two different rockets. One was a **step rocket,** a cluster of rockets strapped together, and the other was a rocket with wings. These drawings predated twentieth century rockets by 300 years. Also in the 1600s, British scientist Isaac Newton explained in his laws of motion how rockets worked by "action and reaction." Exhaust gases shooting backward pushed the rocket forward.

Congreve's rockets

War rockets were noisy and frightening but not as reliable as cannons. In India, Hyder Ali of Mysore used them in the late 1700s to fight the British, and starting in 1808 Sir William Congreve built rockets for the British army. Congreve's rockets had sticks 16 feet (5 meters) long for balance and were fired from metal tubes or A-shaped frames. They had a range of 1 mile (1.8 kilometers). In the 1840s, another British inventor, William Hale, replaced the useless weight of the rocket's stick with curved fins. These made army rockets fly farther and faster.

Soldiers still preferred guns. Small rockets were useful at sea as distress signals and were also fired to carry rescue lines from one ship to another. For most people, however, a rocket was just a firework, an exciting "whoosh" of flame and sparks, vanishing into the night sky. The idea of controlled rocket flight in space seemed as far-fetched as science fiction stories about "men on the Moon."

1000 C.E.	1241	1500	1808	1820s	1840s
The Chinese learn to make gunpowder.	The Tartar army fires rockets at Polish troops.	The first attempt at rocket flight, in China, ends in disaster.	William Congreve invents his artillery rocket, first tried at sea against the French fleet in 1809.	Claudio Ruggiei of Italy fires rats and mice into the air inside rockets.	William Hale improves rocket design by adding fins.

Telescope, 1608

The telescope appeared during the late 1500s, but it is not clear who invented it. In 1608, a Dutch glasses-maker, Hans Lippershey, claimed to have put **lenses** together to invent "an instrument for seeing at a distance." Other inventors also claimed to have made telescopes. The Dutch government rejected Lippershey's claim to be the sole inventor because there were reports of earlier "spyglasses" used by Italian soldiers. Within months, telescopes were being made and sold by lens-makers across Europe.

Stargazing

Italy's greatest scientist, Galileo Galilei, heard about the new invention in 1609 while on a trip to Venice from his home in Padua. As soon as he got home, he ground his own lenses to make a telescope, which he turned skyward to gaze at the stars and planets.

Galileo was the first scientist to look at the Moon and planets through a telescope. What he saw changed people's ideas about the universe.

The Polish **astronomer** Nicolaus Copernicus had already challenged the ancient belief that Earth was the center of the universe. The telescope confirmed his theory about how the planets moved around the sun. Galileo saw the **craters** on the Moon. He also saw **sunspots,** and he discovered the four largest moons of Jupiter **orbiting** the giant planet.

The lens for the eyepiece of Galileo's telescope was **concave.** The farther, or object, lens was **convex.** In 1630, German astronomer Johannes Kepler made a better telescope by fitting convex lenses for both the eyepiece and object lens. This gave a wider field of view and was much better for looking into space.

Refractors and reflectors

Early telescopes worked by **refraction,** which caused blurring and distorted colors. In 1668 Sir Isaac Newton, the great British expert in light and **reflection,** made the first reflecting telescope. It had a metal mirror to collect and focus the light. This solved the blurring and color problems. Later, silvered glass mirrors were used. Today, aluminum is the preferred material.

The first big astronomical telescopes were built in the late 1700s by British astronomer William Herschel. Even bigger ones were made by astronomers in the 1800s. The largest glass lens ever was made in 1897 for the world's biggest refracting telescope at the Yerkes Observatory in California. It has a diameter of 3 feet (1 meter).

Modern telescopes, like this one in Hawaii, are placed on high mountains. The dome slides open when the telescope inside is being used.

Today, city-based optical telescopes cannot get a clear view of the stars because of increasing air pollution. Most telescopes are now on mountaintops, such as Mauna Kea in Hawaii. This is the location for the world's biggest multi-mirror telescope, the Keck. The best site of all is in space, where astronomers can get cloudless views of millions of stars.

1609	1668	1781	1929	1948	1990
Galileo Galilei discovers Jupiter's four largest moons using a telescope.	In England, Sir Isaac Newton builds the first reflecting telescope.	British astronomer William Herschel uses his telescope to discover Uranus.	Bernhard Schmidt of Germany invents a special telescope for photographing large areas of sky.	The Hale reflector telescope in California has a 15-foot (5-meter) mirror.	The first telescope in space, the Hubble Space Telescope, is launched.

Liquid-fueled Rocket, 1926

After Galileo, **astronomers** remained at the forefront of space science until the twentieth century. People could look into space, but they could not get there. Rockets burned a "solid" fuel, **gunpowder.** A gunpowder rocket could only travel through air because its fuel would not burn without **oxygen.** To fly into space, where there is no oxygen, a rocket needed to take its own oxygen, in its fuel.

A Russian dreamer

The first person to suggest that a rocket, burning liquid chemical mixtures that included oxygen, could leave Earth and travel into space was a Russian teacher, Konstantin Tsiolkovski. He spent years calculating how fast a rocket must go to escape from Earth's **gravity.** He tested models in a wind tunnel he built himself before publishing his idea that a rocket firing in stages, one after the other, could break free of Earth's gravity and reach space.

In March 1926, Robert H. Goddard stands beside his rocket, the first to fly on liquid fuel, on his aunt's farm in Massachusetts.

Tsiolkovski never built a rocket. Instead, his books and papers inspired a small band of scientists in other countries, including Hermann Oberth of Germany and Robert Hutchings Goddard of the United States. Space travel was not taken seriously by most scientists. In those days, airplanes were still flimsy cloth-and-wire machines, only just able to cross oceans. Generals were not interested in the long-range rocket **missiles** suggested by Oberth to the German army during World War I. Ignored by governments, the rocket scientists wrote to one another, exchanging ideas.

Goddard's rockets

Robert H. Goddard decided to test a rocket that used petroleum spirit and oxygen, a fuel that would burn even in airless space. In 1920, the *New York Times* newspaper made fun of his suggestion that rockets might one day fly to the Moon. "How could a rocket fly in space," the newspaper article asked, "without any air to push against?" Many people thought that it was a ridiculous notion, but some thought it could be done. In Germany, Hermann Oberth was writing about rockets traveling into space and visiting the planets.

In March 1926, Goddard tested his first rocket, nicknamed Nell, on his aunt's farm, with his wife taking notes. An assistant lit the rocket using a blow torch tied to a long stick! They watched happily as the rocket shot up to a height of about 200 feet (60 meters). Three years later Goddard launched a rocket carrying a camera, **barometer,** and thermometer. In 1935, one of his rockets reached a height of over 6,500 feet (2,000 meters). Goddard had proved that liquid-fueled rockets worked.

Father of the U.S. space program

Although Robert H. Goddard died in 1945, before the first rocket had been fired into space, he is regarded as the father of the U.S. space program. Born in 1882, he worked as a professor of physics and spent his free time building rockets. His results were treated as far-fetched in the U.S. In Germany, however, scientists used Goddard's research to help build the *V-2* missile. In 1962, the Goddard Space Flight Center in Maryland was dedicated in his honor.

1903	1915	1923	1926	1931	1935
Konstantin Tsiolkovski publishes his "rocket into space" theory.	Robert H. Goddard invents the bazooka, a rocket-firing weapon.	In Germany, Hermann Oberth writes a book called *The Rocket into Interplanetary Space.*	In Massachusetts, Robert H. Goddard test-fires the world's first liquid-fueled rocket.	Johannes Winkler of Germany builds a rocket fueled by methane and oxygen.	A "Goddard Rocket" flies faster than sound.

Radio Telescope, 1937

By 1900, scientists were beginning to realize just how big space was. They used optical telescopes to look at visible stars. They knew, too, about other invisible forms of **radiation** given off by stars, including radio waves, X-rays, and infrared rays. New "radio" telescopes that could detect and study these rays told scientists much about the size and age of the universe.

Karl Jansky went to work for the Bell Telephone company in 1928. Three years later, he traced radio signals from the stars.

Scientists became aware of radiation in space in the late 1880s, when inventors such as Heinrich Hertz of Germany began studying radio waves. Work on the radio by the Italian engineer Guglielmo Marconi led to the first radio broadcasts in the early 1900s.

Listening to the crackle of radio signals, engineers came across a puzzle. From time to time, they picked up unusual signals with no known source. Where could these mysterious radio signals be coming from?

Signals from space

Radio signals from space were finally identified in 1931. An American engineer named Karl Jansky was working for Bell Laboratories. His job was to trace mysterious radio signals that interfered with shortwave radio telephone calls to ships at sea. He built a receiver to "listen in" and detected one whistling signal that he picked up four minutes earlier each day. This time-shift coincided with the reappearance of stars. It gave him the clue he needed to track the signal to the star system Sagittarius, millions of miles away. Jansky's discovery caused a sensation, but he was not an **astronomer** and never followed up his breakthrough.

The first radio telescope was made in 1937 by Grote Reber, a Chicago-based astronomer who set up the device in his backyard. Reber was a **"ham radio"** operator and spent most of his spare time and money on his hobby. He set up a dish **antenna** measuring 10 feet (3 meters) across, and after trying for two years, he managed to receive signals from stars. He drew a "radio map" of the Milky Way **galaxy** that was published in 1944.

By the 1950s, astronomers had realized the importance of radio astronomy, and the first big radio telescopes were built. In England in 1957, the Jodrell Bank dish, one of the world's largest radio telescopes, tracked the world's first artificial **satellite**, *Sputnik 1*.

There are 27 mobile dishes on rails in the Y-shaped Very Large Array radio telescope, set up west of Socorro, New Mexico.

Looking for life

One of the most interesting tasks radio astronomers have is to look for signs of life in outer space. The Search for Extraterrestrial Intelligence (SETI) program was set up to listen for radio signals from other worlds and to send signals from Earth to distant stars. The giant 1,000-foot (305-meter) Arecibo radio telescope in Puerto Rico beams signals towards stars 250,000 **light years** away. It will be 50,000 years before any answer comes back!

1904	1937	1957	1960s	1974	1980
Christian Hulsmeyer patents a "radio detector."	In Chicago, Grote Reber builds the first working radio telescope.	Jodrell Bank in England is the world's first big radio telescope, designed by Bernard Lovell.	Radio astronomers discover quasars, the most distant objects detected from Earth.	The radio telescope at Arecibo, Puerto Rico, is made of over 38,000 aluminum sheets covering a hollow in the ground.	The Very Large Array in New Mexico, the world's most powerful radio telescope, is built.

Satellite, 1957

In the 1660s, Sir Isaac Newton described **gravity,** the force that keeps the Moon **orbiting** Earth. By the 1930s, scientists like rocket pioneer Hermann Oberth were trying to figure out how to send artificial "moons" into space. They calculated that a rocket reaching a speed of about seven miles (eleven kilometers) per second would break away from Earth's gravity and go into orbit, becoming a **satellite.** Such satellites could have many uses for communications, for studying space, and for looking down on Earth.

Passersby stare at a model of Sputnik 1, the first artificial satellite. Its launch by the Soviet Union in 1957 made news headlines around the world.

The Soviets launch Sputnik

Launching a satellite required a big rocket. Before 1957, research rockets had reached only the edge of outer space. To launch a satellite, a more powerful, three-stage **step rocket** was needed. As the first and second stages used up their fuel, they separated and fell back to the ground, leaving the final stage to speed on into orbit.

During the 1950s, the **Soviet Union** secretly built very large **missiles** to carry **nuclear weapons.** From these missiles, Soviet rocket builders developed the 330-ton (300-metric-ton) *Vostok* satellite launcher, designed by aircraft engineer Sergei Korolev. On October 4, 1957, this rocket launched a 24-inch (61-centimeter) sphere named *Sputnik* ("Companion") into orbit. The world's first artificial satellite weighed 185 pounds (83 kilograms), and as it circled Earth, its signals were heard by radio listeners all over the world. A month later, a second Soviet satellite was launched. *Sputnik 2* was ten times heavier and carried the first traveler, a dog named Laika, into space.

The space race

The United States had also been building rockets such as the *Aerobee,* designed by James Van Allen. The Soviet Union's success was an enormous shock to the U.S. government. The U.S. satellite program had been held up by rivalry between the army and the air force, each of whom had their own missiles. The United States had pinned its hopes on a much smaller scientific rocket called *Vanguard,* but it was having problems. Suddenly, they found themselves in a "space race" with the Soviets.

A military rocket, the *Jupiter,* was hurriedly modified to launch *Explorer,* the first American satellite, in 1958. The first *Explorer* satellites were designed by Van Allen and his team, and the doughnut-shaped radiation zones they discovered were named the Van Allen Belts.

Later, other countries launched satellites. France was the third nation to do so, followed by China, Japan, and Britain. Some satellites stay in orbit for many years. Others, closer to Earth, burn up as they reenter the atmosphere. The biggest satellite ever recovered from space was the *LDF (Long Duration Exposure Facility),* a bus-sized capsule launched by the United States in 1984 and picked up by the space shuttle *Columbia* in 1990.

1946	1957	1958	1958	1958	1958
James Van Allen works on German V-2 rockets and develops the *Aerobee* research rocket.	Soviet launches of *Sputnik 1* and *Sputnik 2* startle the scientific world.	*Explorer 1,* the first U.S. satellite, is launched by a Jupiter C rocket.	The *Vanguard* rocket launches its fist satellite, discovering the inner layer of the Van Allen radiation belt.	The Soviet *Sputnik 3* is the first multipurpose satellite with an array of scientific instruments.	U.S. government sets up **National Aeronautics and Space Administration (NASA).**

Space Probe, 1959

A **satellite** is held in **orbit** by Earth's **gravity.** To break free of Earth's atmosphere and become a space probe, traveling out to the Moon or the planets, a spacecraft must reach **"escape velocity,"** roughly 25,000 miles (40,000 kilometers) per hour. The **Soviet Union** led the way with *Luna 1* in 1959. The first probe to escape Earth, it sent radio signals from 370,000 miles (597,000 kilometers) away. Six months later, *Luna 2* hit the Moon.

Building a probe

In the 1950s, computers were so big they filled rooms, and cameras and radios were heavy. The invention of the **integrated circuit** by Jack Kilby in 1958 meant that onboard electronic equipment could be made very small. A rocket could send a small "smart" probe zooming out across space to explore the planets.

The Soviet Luna 2 *probe made history, and a new **crater,** in 1959, when it crashed into the Moon.*

The space and arms race drove the Soviet Union and the United States to spend huge amounts of money inventing electronic guidance systems and smaller, more powerful computers. Calculating the course a tiny spacecraft should take on a journey lasting several years was very complicated! The target planet is constantly moving and so is Earth, so the probe has to be sent on a curving path. By the end of the 1960s, the United States had taken the lead in space **electronics.**

Alone in space

A space probe had to be as close to perfect as human engineers could make it. Every system had a backup in case something went wrong. The probe had to work for many months alone in space. It had to carry its own power supply in the form of specially-made batteries, solar cells, or nuclear reactors. It had to be tough enough to withstand the shock of acceleration during launch. It also had to survive in the hostile environment of space.

A space probe did not need a streamlined shape, like a jet plane, since there is no **friction** in space. It could have items sticking out all over it, like solar panels, radio dishes, and antennas. Engineers fitted electronic guidance systems, **gyroscopes** to detect changes in acceleration, and small gas jets or rockets to make steering changes. They installed cameras to photograph the planets and instruments, such as **radiation** detectors, thermometers, and **spectroscopes** to record changing conditions around the probe.

Probes sent back the first pictures of the far side of the Moon. Each complete image was built in strips.

Probes to the planets

The United States and the Soviet Union sent robot probes to the planets Venus and Mars, beginning with *Venera 3* in 1965. **NASA** scientists, such as Carl Sagan, planned trips to Mars and across the **solar system.** Such journeys across millions of miles would take many years. *Pioneer 10* left the solar system in 1983, eleven years after leaving Earth. The *Voyager 2* probe, launched in 1977, visited Jupiter in 1979, Saturn in 1981, Uranus in 1986, and Neptune in 1989. This amazing space explorer is expected to remain "alive" until 2020, periodically sending back data from far beyond the solar system.

1959	1965	1970	1977	1989-1993	1999
The Soviet probe *Luna 1* flies into space beyond Earth's orbit.	The *Mariner 4* probe sends back photographs of Mars.	The Soviet Union's *Venera 7* is the first probe to survive landing on Venus.	*Voyager 1* and *Voyager 2* leave Earth, carrying messages from Earth for any aliens who might find them.	NASA's *Magellan* maps the surface of Venus by **radar.**	The *Galileo* probe orbits Jupiter, studying its four largest moons.

Weather and Resources Satellites, 1960

Scientists quickly realized that a **satellite** in **orbit** could be the perfect "weather station" in space. A satellite could photograph land and sea, providing up-to-the-minute information about crops, drought, and pollution. It could even search for oil or gas hidden underground.

The first aerial photographs were taken from balloons and airplanes. The first weather satellite was launched in 1960, and today the world is ringed by satellites watching the weather and warning of looming environmental problems.

Eyes in the sky

Scientists were delighted with the first satellite photographs of Earth, sent back in 1958. No one could now argue that the world was flat! Satellites revealed that Earth is round. By 1959, satellites were sending back television pictures showing the clouds, oceans, and continents, and the first weather satellite was being built.

Satellites track hurricanes whirling across the ocean. Early warning gives people on land time to evacuate or seek shelter from the storm.

Today, we see satellite weather photos on television, but before 1960, almost all weather information came from ground stations and scattered weather ships at sea. The first weather satellite was called *TIROS* (*Television Infrared Observation Satellite*) and was launched in 1960. It took one photo per hour from a height of 470 miles (750 kilometers). Thousands of photographs were sent back to weather stations on Earth from ten *TIROS* satellites. In the 1970s, bigger *Nimbus* satellites took over. Weather satellites in **geostationary orbit** observe weather patterns, while others fly over the poles so that the whole planet is covered. Their data is analyzed by computers to predict the weather more accurately

> ## How long do satellites last?
> Many satellites end their lives burning up when they reenter Earth's atmosphere after a few years. Some may last almost forever. *LAGEOS* (*Laser Geodynamic Satellite*) is a reflector from which ground stations bounce **lasers** to study continental drift and ocean tides. It orbits so high, almost 3,600 miles (5,800 kilometers) from Earth, that it should remain in orbit for eight million years!

A technician checks TIROS I, the first weather satellite. It was launched in 1960 and was the first of a series of weather satellites.

than ever before. With satellites on watch, hurricanes can be spotted as they form over the ocean, giving time for people in the storm's path to evacuate and seek shelter.

Earth resource satellites

Scientific Earthwatch satellites, such as *OGO-1* (*Orbiting Geophysical Observatory*, launched in 1964), were placed in geostationary orbit. Using **radar,** television, and special cameras, such satellites gave scientists a clearer picture of human use and misuse of the planet's resources.

Landsat 1, launched in 1972, was the first satellite to send back data about farming, forestry, minerals, land use, and water resources. Other Landsats have found new reserves of petroleum, tracked pollution of rivers and lakes, monitored city growth, and warned of floods or droughts. *Seasat* in 1978 and *Geosat* in 1985 used radar to map the ocean and the ocean floor.

1959	1959	1960	1964	1965	1972
The *Vanguard 2* satellite takes the first photographs of clouds covering Earth.	*Explorer 6* sends back the first television pictures of Earth.	*TIROS I* is the first weather satellite.	*OGO-1* is the first orbiting geophysical observatory.	*TIROS 10*, funded by the U.S. weather bureau, has two television cameras to scan Earth's weather.	*Landsat* is the first Earth resources satellite.

Spy and Navigation
Satellites, 1960

The first **satellite** launchers were rockets originally designed to carry **nuclear weapons.** During the **Cold War** of the 1950s and 60s, the United States and the **Soviet Union** spent large sums of money and resources on new weapons. This arms race also sparked off rivalry in space. Both sides launched secret satellites to spy from space. These satellites also served as navigation beacons to guide submarines and aircraft.

Spies in space

During the Cold War, the Soviet Union kept almost all its space research secret. The United States was more open, allowing press and television coverage of most spaceflights, except for secret military missions. The secret spacecraft had cameras and **radar** that could detect very small targets. They were placed in **orbits** that took them over enemy territory to spy on military bases, rocket launch sites, and research centers.

Discoverer 13 returned to Earth in 1960, the first satellite to be recovered from orbit with its data and photos.

Modern spy satellites, such as the U.S. *Crystals,* check that **disarmament** agreements are being properly carried out. Their "electronic eyes" (infrared telescopes and heat-seeking equipment) are so sensitive that they can send back images of objects as small as trees or trucks. Electronic "ferret" satellites can eavesdrop on radio and telephone calls. The U.S. government has plans for a **missile** defense screen that would use satellites and rockets to shoot down enemy missiles.

Navigation satellites

Since ships first sailed the oceans over 5,000 years ago, people have found their way by looking at the stars. When the space age began in 1957, the satellite became an artificial star that could be tracked from the ground.

Navigation satellites can now guide a ship, plane, or even a truck in the desert.

In 1960, the U.S. Navy launched *Transit*, a secret satellite beacon to guide its nuclear submarines. By 1964, there were seven *Transit* satellites orbiting Earth. Radio signals from the satellites are picked up by computerized receivers on ships and submarines.

A later system, developed in the 1990s by the Air Force, is the *NAVSTAR* Global Positioning System (GPS). It uses 24 satellites in orbit around Earth. To find its position, a truck or a ship uses its radio and computer equipment to locate four or more satellites in space. The computer uses this data to pinpoint its position exactly.

Inventing the electronic eye

In 1969, two American **electronics** engineers, Willard Boyle and George Smith, invented a gadget called a charge-coupled device (CCD). It is a chip with a grid containing millions of microscopic light-sensitive pixels, which convert light into electrical signals. **NASA** took up the idea to develop smaller cameras for space use, and the CCD became the "electronic eye" in spy satellites and the Hubble Space Telescope. Its invention led to the development of digital cameras in the 1990s.

How GPS satellites work

A ship in the middle of an ocean can find its position by linking to four or more navigation satellites orbiting in space.

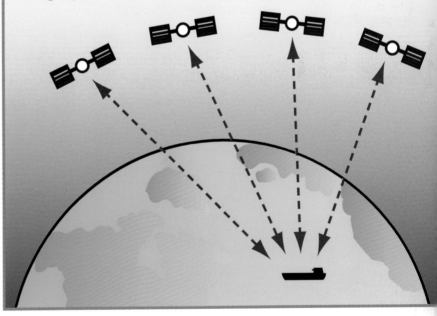

1896	1960	1961	1978	1983	1995
The first ship-to-shore radio signals are sent by Guglielmo Marconi.	The U.S. Navy launches the first *Transit* navigation satellite.	The *Midas* is the first spy satellite able to spot missile launches.	The first NAVSTAR satellite is launched.	The Strategic Defense Initiative, or "Star Wars," is proposed to track and shoot down enemy missiles in space.	The Air Force's NAVSTAR global positioning system is fully operational.

Manned Spacecraft, 1961

The first **satellite,** *Sputnik 1,* showed that it was possible to send craft into space. In 1960, the **Soviet Union** launched a craft carrying two dogs and brought them back safely after 20 hours in space. This illustrated three things. First, Soviet rockets were powerful enough to launch a human-weight **payload.** Second, Soviet engineers had mastered the tricky maneuvers of reentry and landing. And third, their spacecraft had a life-support system able to keep living things alive in space.

Cosmonauts and astronauts

Space flight was presumed to be very demanding physically and mentally. The Soviet Union and United States had been training space fliers since the late 1950s, picking young, fit pilots. It was a jet pilot, Yuri Gagarin, who rocketed into history on April 12, 1961. He was the Soviet Union's first **cosmonaut.** In an historic first, he circled Earth once, in 108 minutes. His brief trip, strapped into his seat inside the cramped *Vostok* capsule, ended with a parachute landing and a hero's welcome. Future flights were planned for Gagarin, but he was killed in a plane crash in 1968.

NASA picked seven pilots as the first **astronauts.** There were no women among them. In the late 1950s, there were very few women jet pilots, and many doctors thought the stresses of space flight would be too severe for a female astronaut. In 1963, Valentina Tereshkova of the Soviet Union proved this was not true, and since her flight, women have made many spaceflights.

*Two dogs named Strelka and Belka were the first animals to return from **orbiting** Earth in Sputnik 5. They landed safely by parachute.*

Success and tragedy in space

The first American manned craft was the cone-shaped *Mercury* capsule, just big enough for one person. The Soviet *Vostok* was three times heavier, but by 1964, the *Voskhod 1* had put three cosmonauts into space together.

In 1965, a Soviet cosmonaut made the first space walk. The dangers of spaceflight were seen in 1967, when the new *Soyuz* spacecraft suffered a fatal accident. Soviet cosmonaut Vladimir Komarov died when the reentry system failed. His landing capsule survived the crash to Earth, but he was killed.

NASA moved on to two-man *Gemini* missions, involving the **docking** of two craft in space. Astronauts perfected reentry and landing techniques, using parachutes to "splash down" into the ocean. Much of this success was due to the work of Robert Gilruth, head of the Manned Spacecraft Center in Houston, Texas. The Gemini program led to the bigger *Apollo* craft. *Apollo 8* flew around the Moon in 1968 and *Apollo 11* landed on the Moon in 1969.

Yuri Gagarin was strapped into the cramped cabin of the Vostok *spacecraft when he circled Earth in 1961. His brief flight turned fantasy into reality. The journey into space had begun and made Gagarin a world hero, though he never flew in space again.*

Robert Gilruth (1913–2000)

Like many space pioneers, Robert Gilruth began as an aircraft engineer. In the 1940s, he worked on **robot** planes, **missiles,** and rocket planes that flew faster than sound. In 1958, he was asked to head the team of scientists at NASA who built the *Gemini* and *Apollo* spacecraft. Gilruth had a knack for picking the right people, and the triumphant *Apollo* moon flights were a testament to the success of his team's work.

1961	1962	1963	1967	1981	1998
Yuri Gagarin of the Soviet Union makes the first manned spaceflight.	NASA astronaut John Glenn is the first American to orbit Earth.	Soviet cosmonaut Valentina Tereshkova is the first woman in space.	Vladmir Komarov is the first person to be killed in space.	First flight of the NASA space shuttle, capable of taking seven astronauts into space.	John Glenn returns to space, becoming the oldest shuttle passenger at the age of 77.

Space Suit, 1961

Illustrations in science fiction stories of the 1800s showed space explorers wearing everyday clothes. By the 1930s, artists were drawing **astronauts** in space suits, for by then scientists had realized that no human could live in space without the protection of special clothing. The modern space suit has come through several stages of design, with engineers, doctors, and the astronauts themselves all working together.

Suits under water and in the air

The first "space suits" were deep-sea diving suits, invented in the 1800s. These were airtight as well as waterproof, with a metal helmet. The divers breathed through air hoses. In the 1930s, the first "pressure suits" were worn by high-altitude pilots and balloonists. Above 65,000 feet (20,000 meters), pilots must wear pressure suits to keep the fluids in their bodies moving. In the late 1940s, the first **supersonic** pilots, such as Chuck Yeager, risked becoming unconscious if they flew without pressure suits. When the human body is stressed by rapid acceleration, the supply of blood to the brain may be slowed down or cut off.

In the 1960s, test pilots flew the X-15 rocket plane so fast and so high that they needed to wear pressure suits, like astronauts do.

Life support in space

The first person to wear a space suit in space was Soviet **cosmonaut** Yuri Gagarin in 1961, although he never left the safety of his cabin. Not until 1965 did people venture outside a spacecraft, floating in space with only a space suit for protection. The first suits were not very different from air force flying suits and were not easy to move in. The moon suits developed by **NASA** designers for the *Apollo* astronauts between 1969 and 1972 were more comfortable, with rubber joints for walking and bending. The suits were liquid-cooled. They were made of layers of nylon and other **synthetic** materials and had a tough outer layer of teflon-coated glass fiber.

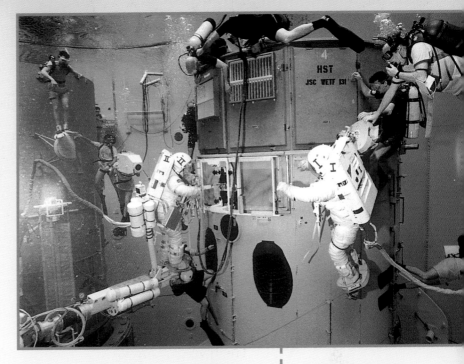

Shuttle suits

Since the 1980s, designers have developed new clothing for astronauts working on space stations or space shuttles. Inside, they usually work in regular shirts and pants. Outside the spacecraft, an astronaut must wear a space suit. The space suit's life-support system supplies them with pure **oxygen** to breathe. On Earth, we breathe a mixture of nitrogen and oxygen. The suit has several layers to protect the wearer from **radiation** and to prevent the suit from being punctured by flying dust particles. The suits are reusable and come in interchangeable parts, made in different sizes, so they can be assembled for each mission to fit both large and small astronauts.

To train for space walks, astronauts in space suits practiced underwater in giant tanks. Floating felt like zero gravity.

On the chest is a control pad and toolkit. The inner suit has heating elements to keep the wearer warm and water-filled tubes to keep him or her cool in the full sun. The helmet's gold-tinted visor is scratch-resistant and shades the eyes from the blinding sunlight. Underneath, the astronaut wears a cap containing a personal radio. The suit comes with a built-in waste-disposal system, in case the wearer needs to go to the bathroom. Though heavier than the astronaut on the ground, it is feather-light in the weightlessness of space.

1930s	1947	1961	1965	1969	1971
Pressure suits are tested by pilots in planes and balloons.	Chuck Yeager of the United States makes the first supersonic flight.	Yuri Gagarin of the Soviet Union becomes the first person in space to wear a space suit all the time.	Soviet cosmonaut Aleksei Leonov becomes the first "space walker."	*Apollo* astronauts walk and work on the Moon protected by their space suits.	Race car driver Richard Petty wears a water-cooled suit based on space suit technology.

Moon Rocket, 1969

The giant rocket that took the first **astronauts** to the Moon in 1969 was a direct development of World War II **missiles** that were designed to bomb cities. The brain behind **NASA's** *Saturn 5* moon rocket belonged to German engineer Wernher von Braun. As a young rocket builder in the 1930s, von Braun dreamed of giant space rockets. In 1934, he designed the *A-2*, a rocket fueled by ethyl alcohol and liquid **oxygen.**

A Saturn 5 launches as the first stage engines lift it slowly off the ground.

The V-2 missile

When World War II began in 1939, von Braun went to work at the top secret rocket research base at Peenemünde in northern Germany. In 1942, his team built the *A-4* rocket, which flew at five times the speed of sound and soared to the edge of space. Renamed the *V-2*, this rocket became a deadly weapon, showering down on London and other European cities without warning. Fortunately, the new weapon came too late to prevent Germany's defeat. By 1945, Peenemünde had been destroyed by bombing, and many German scientists, plans, and rocket parts were seized by the Allies.

Building the moon rocket

Von Braun went to the United States and began designing new rockets based on the *V-2*. Some were army missiles, but von Braun wanted to build space rockets big enough to send spacecraft into **orbit** around Earth, and to the Moon and back.

Von Braun helped launch the first U.S. **satellite** in 1958, but he realized that the Russians had a big lead in the space race. President John F. Kennedy promised that the nation would land astronauts on the Moon before the 1960s ended, a huge challenge for von Braun and the other NASA engineers. At great speed, they built the biggest rocket in the world, the *Saturn 5*.

The *Saturn 5* had eleven separate engines in three stages, weighed 6 million pounds (2.7 million kilograms), and was over 360 feet (110 meters) tall. The ground shook as it lifted from the launchpad, burning over 50,000 gallons (2 million liters) of fuel in the first 2.5 minutes of flight. It sent six spacecraft to the Moon between 1969 and 1972 and also launched the space laboratory, *Skylab*.

Successors to Saturn

When the *Apollo* and *Skylab* programs ended in 1973, the giant rocket was no longer needed. NASA turned its attention to the reusable space shuttle in 1981. However, big rockets are still used for satellite launches. Modern ones include the American *Atlas* and *Delta* launchers, China's *Long March* rocket, and the European Space Agency's *Ariane*.

Wernher von Braun (1912–1977)

Wernher von Braun was born in Wirsitz, Germany (now part of Poland). He read Hermann Oberth's book *The Rocket Into Interplanetary Space*, and later built small model rockets. During World War II, von Braun and General Walter Dornberger were put in charge of the rocket plant at Peenemünde. When the war ended, von Braun went to the United States and in 1955 he became a U.S. citizen. The 1969 *Apollo 11* mission saw his dream come true, sending people to the Moon. Von Braun left NASA in 1972 and died in 1977.

1944	1949	1958	1969	1973	1981
German *V-2* rockets are fired against Antwerp and London.	The *Viking* launcher, an improved version of the *V-2*, is built.	The first U.S. satellite, *Explorer I*, is launched by a *Jupiter* rocket.	A *Saturn 5* rocket sends *Apollo 11* to the Moon. The **Soviet Union's** *N-1* moon rocket blows up.	A *Saturn 5* rocket launches the *Skylab* space station.	The first space shuttle mission is launched, without the aid of a *Saturn 5*.

Moon Lander, 1969

In the 1960s, every space explorer looked toward the Moon. The United States spent billions of dollars building a craft able to land people on the Moon and return them to Earth. They made it in 1969. When **astronauts** will return to the Moon, no one knows.

The moon race

The Soviet probe *Luna 2* crashed onto the Moon in September 1959. A month later, *Luna 3* took the first photographs of the far side of the Moon. Because of its **rotation,** the Moon always shows the same side to people on Earth.

By 1960, **NASA** engineers were planning to build the huge *Saturn 5* rocket to send a three-man craft from Earth to the Moon. Most Americans believed they were in a race with the **Soviet Union** to put people on the Moon. Hundreds of companies were involved in the project, making thousands of components such as fuel cells, **electronics,** cameras, life-support systems, engines, and space suits. Every part had to be tested hundreds of times—one failure, and three astronauts would be stranded in space.

Neil Armstrong and Edwin "Buzz" Aldrin were the first people to walk on the Moon. They performed many experiments, such as this one, to measure seismic ("moonquake") activity during their lunar landing.

To seek suitable landing sites, unmanned craft were sent to the Moon. The American *Ranger* craft was launched in 1964 and 1965 to send back close-up pictures. In 1966, the Soviet *Luna 9* made the first **soft landing** on the Moon and sent back the first television pictures. To test landing techniques, NASA sent *Surveyor 3* to the Moon in 1967. *Lunar Orbiters* circled the Moon, descending to heights of 28 miles (45 kilometers) to photograph possible landing sites.

The *Apollo* moon mission

Thousands of people worked on the *Apollo* craft. It had three sections. The command **module** was the control center and living quarters. It was the only part to return to Earth. The service module contained rocket engines and fuel. The lunar module was the only part intended to land on the Moon. It looked flimsy, with spidery legs and paper-thin metal skin. It was only meant for two people. The third astronaut would remain inside the **orbiting** command module.

The *Apollo* program suffered a terrible setback in 1967 when a fire killed three astronauts on the ground. The first manned *Apollo* flight did not take place until October 1968. Just two months later, three astronauts flew around the Moon in *Apollo 8*. In March 1969, *Apollo 9* tested the lunar module in Earth's orbit. Next, in May 1969, came a practice run for a landing, as *Apollo 10* orbited the Moon, dropping to 9 miles (14.5 kilometers) above the surface, but not landing. In July 1969, *Apollo 11* repeated the performance. This time the lunar module landed, and for the first time people walked on the surface of the Moon.

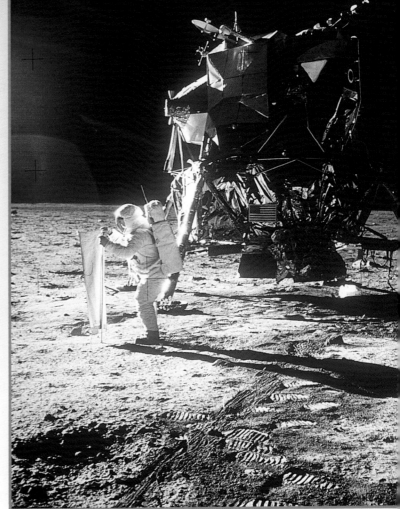

The flag and footprints left on the Moon by the Apollo *11 crew were not disturbed by any movement on the airless, weatherless Moon.*

1850s	1959	1961	1968	1969	1972
The first photographs of the Moon are taken from Earth.	The Soviet Union's *Luna 2* is the first probe to hit the Moon.	President Kennedy promises to land Americans on the Moon before the end of the decade.	*Apollo 8* flies around the Moon and returns safely to Earth.	*Apollo 11* astronauts Neil Armstrong and "Buzz" Aldrin land on the Moon.	*Apollo 17* is the last *Apollo* moon mission.

Space Rover, 1970

Many scientists argued against sending **astronauts** to the Moon. Send machines instead, they said. Machines don't need air or food. Space rovers did go to the Moon and to Mars. They showed that many useful scientific experiments can be done by **robot** machines, programmed by computer and controlled by radio from Earth.

Robots and rovers on the Moon

Robot explorers were first tried on the Moon in 1970. When the **Soviet Union's** *Luna 16* craft landed on the Moon, from it emerged an eight-wheeled vehicle, the first robot to explore the Moon. Known as *Lunokhod*, the solar-powered robot carried television cameras and a small X-ray telescope. It could use its remotely controlled arms to examine rocks. It rolled a total distance of more than 6 miles (10 kilometers) during a five-month mission, surviving the freezing cold of the lunar night.

The lunar rover had four-wheel drive and could travel 7 miles (11 kilometers) an hour. Astronauts could use the rover to carry equipment over the Moon.

On the last three **NASA** moon landings (*Apollos 15, 16,* and *17*), the astronauts "unfolded" the remarkable lunar rover. This electric car traveled at a top speed of 9 miles (14 kilometers) per hour and carried twice its own weight. The average car carries only half its weight. The four-wheel drive of the moon buggy used a new lubricant system invented by engineer John B. Christian. It kept the wheels turning smoothly in any temperature, from freezing cold to scorching hot. The buggy was steered by a T-shaped controller, not a steering wheel. Riding allowed the astronauts to explore more of the Moon and save precious **oxygen** and water.

Robots on Mars

A manned flight to Mars and back will be long and difficult, but robots have already begun to explore the planet. In 1997, the *Pathfinder* spacecraft released the small *Sojourner* vehicle, the first rover to explore another planet. It weighed about 9 pounds (4 kilograms) on Mars and crawled at 25 inches (60 centimeters) a minute, never straying further than 33 feet (10 meters). *Sojourner* had six wheels to make climbing easier and a solar panel for electric power. It worked for three months until its parent craft got too cold and "died."

In 2003, NASA plans to launch the *Mars Exploration Rover*. Two probes will make a bouncy landing on Mars, cushioned by air bags, and release two robot rovers. Each rover will cover 330 feet (100 meters) during a Martian day.

The little Sojourner *robot rolled up to examine rocks near the* Pathfinder *lander. It found evidence of water long ago on Mars.*

The first moon drivers

The first people to drive on another world were astronauts David Scott and James Irwin in July 1971. Their twelve-day *Apollo 15* mission included two trips in the lunar rover, which at first proved hard to steer, a real "bucking bronco" in the Moon's weak **gravity.** They needed their seat belts! Both astronauts fell over while exploring on foot but found that the improved space suits they were wearing made getting up easier.

1969	1970	1971	1972	1997
The ALSEP scientific set-up is left on the Moon by *Apollo 12*.	The Soviet *Lunokhod* is the first robot explorer on the Moon.	*Apollo 15* lands the first of three lunar rovers.	The third and last lunar rover is left on the Moon.	*Pathfinder's Sojourner* robot crawls on Mars studying rocks.

Space Food and Fitness, 1971

The first **astronauts** were all young, fit pilots. Today's space travelers enjoy greater comfort and do not have to undergo such strenuous training. Special food and advances in space medicine make sure that astronauts stay healthy while in space.

In 1961, Yuri Gagarin spent less than two hours in space and did not eat, wash, or sleep. As humans made longer flights, lasting up to a year, scientists had to solve the "housekeeping" and fitness problems caused by long stays in space. The launch of the **Soviet Union's** space station *Salyut* in 1971 began the new era of making spaceflight safer and more comfortable.

Eating in space

Because everything is weightless in space, eating and drinking present problems. Liquid floats out of a cup and crumbs float around a cabin. Food trays and cutlery would float around too, unless held in place by suction cups, magnets, Velcro, or tape.

Eating and drinking are a welcome, and sometimes amusing, part of daily routine for astronauts on long stays in space.

Freeze-dried food was invented by E. W. Flosdorff in 1947. At first it was just coffee and orange juice. Most space food goes into space frozen or dried and is defrosted or **rehydrated** before eating. Drinks are usually squirted into the mouth or sipped through straws.

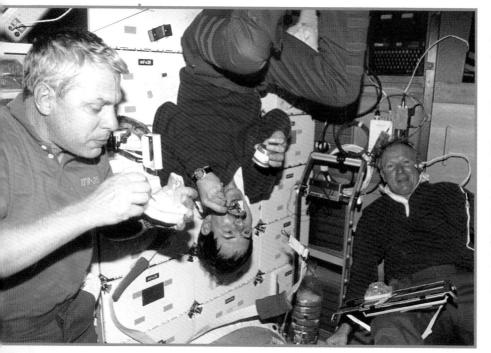

Following the example of airlines, which started serving precooked, prefrozen meals in 1945, space planners know that appetizing meals are important for keeping the astronauts happy. Menus are carefully planned.

On a typical working day in space, shuttle astronauts breakfast on orange juice and scrambled eggs. Lunch might be soup, a sandwich, and a banana. Dinner at the end of the working day might be steak, vegetables, and a dessert.

Health and hygiene

To sleep, astronauts zip themselves into sleeping bags. Velcro, invented by Swiss engineer Georges de Mestral in 1957, is useful for keeping things in place. For extra warmth, astronauts have blankets made of metal foil.

Taking a bath is difficult in space. Water is too precious to be allowed to fly around the spacecraft. Astronauts take a shower inside a sealed unit. The space shower, which reuses or recycles 93 percent of the water, was invented by **NASA** engineer Russell Garcia. Toilets are vacuum-operated to suck away the waste—no flushing in space!

About half of all astronauts suffer from space sickness. Mae Jemison, the first African American woman in space, studied motion sickness in zero gravity. She found that meditation techniques helped. Colds can also be a problem. A runny nose is no joke when you are weightless. Better diets and medicines help keep astronauts healthy. Astronauts also exercise every day on machines to make their muscles work. Without **gravity,** muscles have nothing to push and pull against. They begin to waste away after weeks in space. Bones, too, become weaker because of calcium loss. Some of the first astronauts could hardly stand when they returned to Earth.

1961	**1963**	**1971**	**1985**	**1987**	**1995**
Yuri Gagarin proves that a human can survive in space.	Valentina Tereshkova of the Soviet Union is the first woman in space.	The Soviet *Salyut* is the first space station with a refrigerator and fresh water stored in rubber containers.	U.S. Senator Jake Garn is first civilian politician in space.	Yuri Romanenko completes 326 days in space .25 in. (1cm) taller and with 15 percent smaller leg muscles.	Valery Polyakov completes a record-breaking 437-day stay on the *Mir* space station.

Space Station, 1971

The world's first space station, a permanent base for **astronauts** in **orbit** above Earth, was the **Soviet Union's** *Salyut 1*. Its inventors were the engineers who had designed the successful *Soyuz* spacecraft and the *Cosmos* **satellites.**

Long space flights were needed to perform scientific studies. To do this, astronauts had to spend several weeks in orbit, living inside a space laboratory or space station. In the future, space stations will also act as assembly points to build large spacecraft setting out on long voyages to the planets. Doctors monitor space station astronauts to learn how the human body adapts to long periods in space. They also study the effects of space travel on other living things.

Longer and longer space flights

The first manned spacecraft in 1961 spent only a few hours in orbit, but in June 1970 the Soviet *Soyuz 9* completed a flight of almost eighteen days. The first space station, *Salyut 1*, was launched in April 1971. Three **cosmonauts** were killed during their return trip to Earth after the first 23-day stay on *Salyut 1*. Despite this setback, however, by 1983 a further six *Salyuts* had been launched.

This 1995 photo shows a visiting shuttle (bottom) docked with the Mir space station.

Salyut 6 in 1977 had two **docking** ports, so it could be resupplied and refueled by either manned or **robot** spacecraft. *Salyut 7* in 1982 was even more successful. Long-stay cosmonauts spent over 300 days inside it. They received visits from *Soyuz* craft carrying fresh cosmonauts and from unmanned *Progress* craft ferrying supplies.

NASA decided to make use of leftover *Apollo* equipment to build their own space station, called *Skylab*. This orbital laboratory, weighing 95 tons (85 metric tons), was launched by a *Saturn 5* rocket in 1973. It was visited by three teams of astronauts, the last team spending 84 days in space. It carried a spider, nicknamed Arabella, that spun shapeless webs in zero **gravity.** There were also minnows, which swam in a spiral motion. *Apollo* astronauts had suffered from colds and space sickness, but the *Skylab* flights showed that with exercise and better food, astronauts could stay healthy and work for long periods.

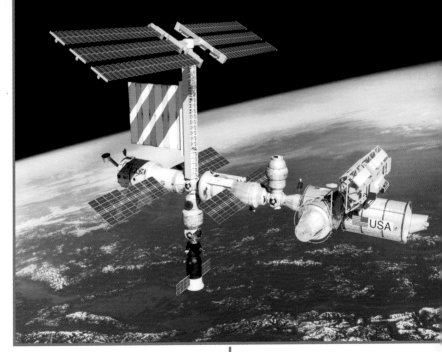

The International Space Station Alpha is made up of sections assembled in orbit. It will be a permanent platform in space for science. The wing-like solar panels turn sunlight into electrical energy.

Mir and the *ISS*

In 1986, the Soviets launched *Mir*, a much bigger station with six docking ports and room for six astronauts. It stayed in space until 2001. Even bigger will be the International Space Station, now being assembled in orbit. Work started in 1998 with the launch of two **modules,** one American and one Russian. Other parts are being built in Europe, Japan, and Canada. The station will be visible in the night sky. You can access NASA's "Skywatch" Internet site to find out when and where to look for it.

The International Space Station
The first crew of the International Space Station (ISS) were an American, Bill Shepherd, and two Russians, Yuri Gidzenko and Sergei Kinalev. In 2000, they celebrated the first Christmas in space by an *ISS* crew with **rehydrated** turkey. Four crews are now training. Each will spend 90 days aboard the space station. By 2003, the *ISS* should be complete, as new sections are brought up from Earth.

1971	1973	1983	1986	2001
Soviet *Salyut 1* is world's first space station.	NASA launches *Skylab*.	NASA launches *Spacelab*.	The Soviet Union launches the *Mir* space station.	Astronauts are at work on the *ISS Alpha*. *Mir* burns up as it reenters Earth's atmosphere.

Mars Lander, 1976

Mars is the only planet whose surface can be seen from Earth. Thick clouds surround Venus, our other near neighbor in the **solar system.** As it **orbits** the sun, Mars comes within 35 million miles (56 million kilometers) of Earth. To get there by spacecraft takes about six months.

Mars has fascinated scientists and science fiction writers since 1877, when an Italian **astronomer** named Schiaparelli was reported as seeing "canals" on the planet. He actually meant channels, lines on the dry surface, but the English word "canals" suggested civilization, and many people were eager to believe in Martians! In 1898, H. G. Wells wrote of an invasion from Mars in his best-selling book *War of the Worlds.*

Going to Mars

In the early 1960s, **NASA** started planning a manned Mars landing. In 1969, Vice President Agnew spoke of a landing "by the end of the century," and NASA added a date for the expedition, 1982. It has not yet happened.

In 1976, the Viking landers sent back the first pictures of Mars taken from the surface. The photos showed a reddish, rock-strewn desert.

For now, **robots** are the best way to explore Mars. NASA sent the first unmanned probes to Mars in 1965. In 1971, *Mariner 9* orbited the planet at a height of 1,000 miles (1,600 kilometers). From these missions, scientists learned much more about the planet's atmosphere, its two small moons, and its polar ice caps.

Landing on Mars

Mars has a thin atmosphere. It also has a rocky, dusty surface, and landing can be tricky. A spacecraft must descend slowly from orbit, using braking rockets and finally relying on parachutes or inflated air bags to soften the landing. The first **soft landing** on Mars was made by the Soviets in 1971. Their *Mars 3* orbiter released a capsule, but it stopped sending signals after only 20 seconds.

Two Viking *spacecraft like this one landed on Mars in 1976, after a ten-month journey from Earth.* Vikings 1 *and 2 landed about 4,000 miles (6,500 kilometers) apart.*

Scientists got their first close-up look at Mars in 1976, when the NASA space probes *Viking 1* and *2* landed safely using parachutes. They sent back photographs of a windswept desert with sand dunes and sharp rocks. In one photo some people thought they could see a huge "face" carved in the rock. Clearer photos in 1998 by the *Mars Global Surveyor* probe showed that the face was a natural feature, shaped by the wind. In 1997, the *Pathfinder* lander placed the first robot explorer on Mars, the six-wheeled *Sojourner* crawler.

Life on Mars?

Scientists know that Mars is cold and has no **oxygen**. So far, scientific tests on its soil have failed to reveal any signs of life, now or in the past. A claim in 1996 that fossil bacteria had been found in Mars rocks was not accepted by all scientists. Scientists want to send spacecraft to look for water on Mars. If water still exists, there might once have been life on Mars. Perhaps future **astronauts** will be able to use Martian water or mine chemicals to make rocket fuel for the return trip.

1969	1971	1976	1988	1998
The *Mariner 6* probe reveals that Mars has craters, like the Moon.	*Mariner 9* orbits Mars and finds that it is covered by a huge dust storm.	*Viking 1* and 2 land on Mars.	Two Soviet probes to Mars' moon, Phobos, fail.	The *Mars Climate Orbiter* burns up entering Martian atmosphere because of an engineering mistake.

Space Shuttle, 1981

The space shuttle is the cargo truck of space. It flies up into **orbit,** carrying **satellites,** people, space station equipment, and scientific experiments. Unlike a rocket, this winged spacecraft can be used again and again.

Into space and back again

Inventors have designed "rocket planes" to fly into space and back again. In comic books and space movies, rockets usually shoot straight up into space and land back on Earth, often tail first, belching smoke and flames. A real space rocket cannot do this. When a rocket re-enters the atmosphere, it glows red-hot as it meets the **friction** from the air. As it drops lower, it needs parachutes to slow its descent, unless it has wings and can glide down like an airplane.

The space shuttle has a huge cargo bay and an extending mechanical arm for releasing and capturing satellites.

The space liner

In the 1970s, **NASA** engineers built the first winged spacecraft, the space shuttle. It first flew in 1981. About the size of a medium-sized jet plane, the shuttle takes off vertically, attached to a giant fuel tank filled with liquid hydrogen and liquid **oxygen.** Two solid fuel rocket boosters provide extra power for takeoff. They drop off when empty and fall back to Earth for reuse. The spacecraft roars on, burning the fuel in its big tank, which also falls away while the shuttle flies into orbit about 186 miles (300 kilometers) above Earth.

To survive the fierce heat of reentry, the shuttle is shielded by ceramic tiles that absorb the heat. As it meets the air, it begins to gain lift from its wings and glides down to land on a runway.

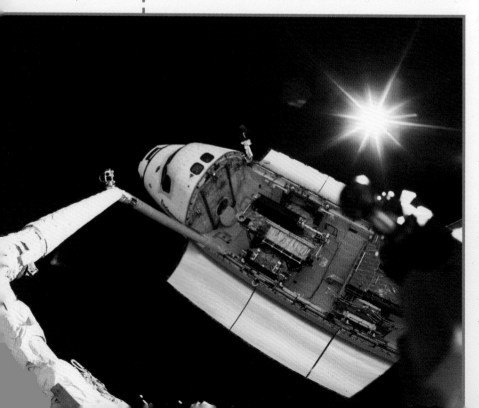

Aside from the devastating *Challenger* disaster in 1986, the shuttle has proved very reliable. The United States has a fleet of four craft.

In the future, smaller shuttle craft, such as the proposed *X-38* crew return vehicle, could serve as "rescue ships" to pick up **astronauts** from the International Space Station, should an emergency arise. In the 1980s, the **Soviet Union** also designed a shuttle, known as *Buran*, which was to be launched by the huge *Energia* rocket. However, this program was abandoned.

Sally Ride, seen here inside the shuttle Challenger in 1983, was the first woman astronaut from the United States. During the six-day flight, she helped launch two satellites and tested the remote manipulator arm. She made a second shuttle flight in 1984.

Sally Ride (b. 1951)

Sally Ride was the third woman and the first American woman in space. Born in California in 1951, she studied physics at Stanford University. In 1979 she was assigned to the shuttle program and in 1983 she made her first flight aboard *Challenger*. It was the first five-person mission. She was back in orbit the following year, also on *Challenger*, and this time one of a record seven-person crew. She later served on the commission that investigated the 1986 explosion that destroyed *Challenger* and killed seven astronauts. In 1987, she left NASA to continue her academic life as a scientist.

1981	1986	1988	1988	1990	1998
The first shuttle mission, by *Columbia*, is launched.	The *Challenger* shuttle explodes, killing all seven crew members.	Shuttle flights resume after changes in design.	Trials begin of the Soviet *Buran* shuttle. It is later abandoned.	A space shuttle launches the Hubble Space Telescope.	A space shuttle launches the first U.S. section of the International Space Station.

Jet Pack, 1984

To get around in space, weightless and airless, an **astronaut** must become a miniature spacecraft. She needs a personal propulsion and guidance system, or jet pack.

The first astronauts did not move from their cramped capsules. By the mid-1960s, scientists were eager to see how well people could work in space, leaving the craft and venturing outside protected only by their space suits.

The first space walks

The first person to try a space walk was Soviet **cosmonaut** Aleksei Leonov. In March 1965, he emerged from the air lock of *Voskhod 2* and spent ten minutes outside, tied to the spacecraft by a safety line. *Gemini 4* astronaut Ed White repeated the feat in June 1965. He experimented with a small handheld "gas gun" to push himself around. The gun was like a water pistol that fired gas. This was the first American extra-vehicular activity (EVA), the **NASA** term for walking in space.

To do work in space, such as setting up experiments and doing repairs, astronauts need freedom to move about easily. In zero **gravity,** every move has to be made with care. Pushing against the side of the craft can cause an astronaut to begin to drift away. In the same way, a jet of gas squirted in one direction produces a force in the opposite direction. A propulsion system for floating in space needed to be simple and reliable—one mistake could send an astronaut flying off into empty space with no hope of rescue.

*U.S. astronaut Ed White floats in space during his 21-minute space walk in 1965. He is holding his **oxygen**-powered "gas gun."*

A narrow escape

EVAs can be dangerous, so astronauts maintain a close watch on any colleague working outside. Soviet cosmonaut Yuri Romanenko had a narrow escape in 1977 during his first flight aboard *Soyuz 26*. He left the cabin for a space walk but failed to check that his safety line was secured. Romanenko would have floated off into space had his quick-thinking partner Georgi Grechko not grabbed the line and hauled him in.

The MMU

In the 1980s, NASA engineers developed a "flying chair," known as the Manned Maneuvering Unit, or MMU, for use on shuttle missions. It was first tried by astronaut Bruce McCandless in February 1984. He wore it for 90 minutes, flying completely free of the shuttle more than 200 miles (350 kilometers) above the Pacific Ocean. He was able to move gently in any direction, firing short bursts of nitrogen gas from the unit's eight sets of thrusters. An astronaut steers the MMU with hand controllers in the "arms." Nitrogen gas is stored in tanks in the backpack. The MMU has no safety line, so the astronaut's life depends entirely on the reliability of its systems.

*Astronauts of the twenty-first century fly free, using the MMU, the fastest "armchair" in or out of this world. While using the MMU, the astronaut becomes a living satellite, traveling around the world at the same speed as the spacecraft to which he or she returns when the space walk is over. Astronauts use their jet packs to move around outside the spacecraft, working on **satellites** or sections of space station.*

1965	1965	1984	1984	1990s	2001
Aleksei Leonov of the **Soviet Union** makes the first space walk.	Astronaut Ed White tries out a handheld "space gun" to help him move around in weightlessness.	Svetlana Savitskaya of the Soviet Union is the first woman to walk in space.	Shuttle astronaut Bruce McCandless tries out the Manned Maneuvering Unit (MMU).	Shuttle astronauts move around the shuttle cargo bay to launch satellites and recover broken ones for repair.	Space shuttle crews use MMUs while assembling the new International Space Station.

Space Telescope, 1990

Telescopes have been around for hundreds of years. They have become less useful on Earth, however, because of the pollution created by city lights, car exhaust, factory smoke, and television signals. To get a really clear view of the stars and planets, scientists send telescopes and other instruments into space itself.

Astronauts work on the Hubble Space Telescope during the 1993 shuttle mission that successfully repaired Hubble's faulty "eye."

Looking for heat in space

The first infrared telescope for use in astronomy was invented by Frank J. Low in 1961. It warmed up slightly every time it detected infrared rays from outer space. An infrared telescope was sent into space on board the *Infrared Astronomy Satellite* (*IRAS*) in 1983, and it began searching for distant stars so cold they give off no visible light. It found over 200,000 infrared sources in the ten months it worked. An infrared telescope like *IRAS* has to be cooled almost to absolute zero or -459°F (-273°C) so that no "haze" of heat from the telescope interferes with the heat rays it is picking up from distant stars.

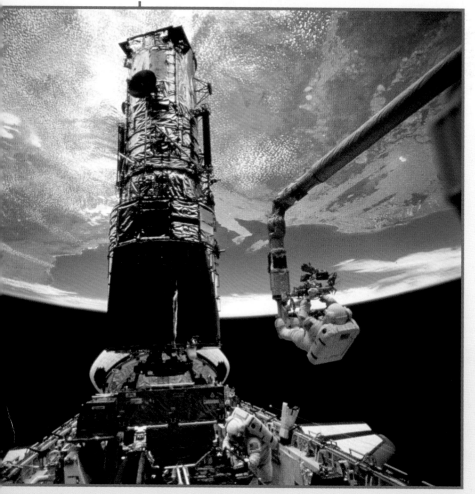

The Hubble Space Telescope

The biggest space telescope yet is the Hubble Space Telescope. Named after **astronomer** Edwin Hubble, it is as big as a truck. It was placed in **orbit** about 370 miles (600 kilometers) above Earth by the shuttle *Discovery* in 1990. It circles Earth about every 90 minutes.

Hubble was designed to send back pictures of stars ten times clearer than the biggest telescopes on Earth can provide. Astronomers were disappointed when the first pictures came back fuzzy. They soon discovered that the telescope's mirror was flawed. At the factory, it had been ground to the wrong shape—a very costly mistake! At first, engineers did their best to enhance, or sharpen, the pictures, using computers to correct the fuzzy images. Then, it was decided to "recapture" and repair Hubble. This was done in 1993 by sending the space shuttle *Endeavor* to intercept the giant telescope in orbit. The *Endeavor's* crew succeeded in installing a new device with ten tiny mirrors and a new camera to correct the fault in the mirror. Hubble began sending back brilliant pictures, more detailed than any that could be taken from Earth.

Thanks to the engineers' quick thinking, Hubble gives astronomers on Earth their clearest view yet of the universe. It can peer into the heart of **galaxies,** looking for evidence of **black holes.** It has taken pictures of stars more than 100 million **light years** away from us. Even bigger space telescopes with mirrors designed to unfold up to 26 feet (8 meters) across will be launched in the next few years.

Edwin Hubble (1889–1953)

As a young student, Edwin Hubble was inspired to study the stars by astronomer George E. Hale, who has a large land-based telescope in California named after him. Working at the Mount Wilson Laboratory in California, Hubble discovered that distant galaxies are moving away from us at an increasing speed. Before this discovery, scientists had thought the universe was static, or unchanging. Hubble's observations and calculations showed that it was expanding, probably as a consequence of the Big Bang, the explosion of energy in which the universe began.

1958	1962	1973	1983	1990	1999
Explorer I makes the first astronomical observations from space.	The *Orbiting Solar Observatory* is launched to study radiation from the Sun.	The *Apollo* telescope mount is carried on the *Skylab* space station.	IRAS (*Infrared Astronomy Satellite*) finds new stars.	The Hubble Space Telescope is the first large telescope in space.	The European XMM (X-ray multi-mirror) telescope is launched by an *Ariane* rocket.

Timeline

1000 C.E. By this date, the Chinese have learned how to make **gunpowder.**

1241 The Tartar army fires rockets at Polish troops. This is the first recorded use of rocket warfare.

1609 Galileo discovers Jupiter's four largest moons with the aid of his telescope.

1668 Sir Isaac Newton builds the first reflector telescope, with a mirror to collect light.

1850s The first photographs of the Moon are taken from Earth by William C. Bond and J. A. Whipple of Harvard University.

1926 Robert Goddard test fires the world's first liquid-fueled rocket.

1935 A "Goddard" rocket flies faster than sound.

1937 Grote Reber builds the first working radio telescope.

1957 The **Soviet Union** launches the first **satellites,** *Sputnik 1* and *Sputnik 2.*

1958 *Explorer 1,* the first **NASA** satellite, is launched by a *Jupiter C* rocket.

1959 A Soviet space probe, *Luna 2,* is the first to hit the Moon.

1960s Radio **astronomers** discover quasars, the most distant objects detected from Earth.

1960 *TIROS 1,* the first weather satellite, is launched.

1960 The first *Transit* Navigation Satellite is launched.

1961 Yuri Gagarin flies into history on *Vostok 1,* the world's first manned spacecraft.

1963 Soviet **cosmonaut** Valentina Tereshkova becomes the first woman in space.

1965	Aleksei Leonov is the first person to make a space walk wearing a space suit.
1969	A *Saturn 5* rocket sends the *Apollo 11* spacecraft on its historic trip to the Moon.
	Apollo 11 **astronauts** Neil Armstrong and Edwin "Buzz" Aldrin land on the Moon.
1970	The Soviet Union's *Lunokhod* is the first **robot** explorer on the Moon, and its *Venera 7* is the first probe to survive landing on Venus.
1971	The Soviet Union's *Salyut 1* is the world's first space station.
1972	*Landsat*, the first earth-resources satellite, is launched.
1976	*Viking 1* lands on Mars on July 20. *Viking 2* follows on September 3.
1978	The United States launches the first *Navstar* satellites, setting up a global navigation system.
1981	The first space shuttle mission, by *Columbia*, is completed.
1984	Shuttle astronaut Bruce McCandless tests the Manned Maneuvering Unit (MMU).
1986	The *Challenger* space shuttle explodes 73 seconds after takeoff, killing all seven crew members.
	The Soviets launch the *Mir* Space Station.
1990	The Hubble Space Telescope, the first large telescope in space, is launched.
1995	Valery Polyakov completes 439 days on *Mir*, the longest stay in space to date.
1997	The *Sojourner* robot crawls on Mars, studying rocks.
2001	Astronauts are at work on board the International Space Station, which is being assembled in stages.

Glossary

antenna device for collecting electrical and radio signals

astronaut person trained to fly in space

astronomer scientist who studies the stars and other objects in space

barometer instrument for measuring air pressure

black hole all that remains of a collapsed star. It is a tiny object with such great mass that not even light can escape the pull of its gravity, so it is invisible.

Cold War period of hostility between the West (the U.S and its allies) and the Communist world (Soviet Union and China and their allies), which lasted from the 1940s to the 1980s

concave curved shape like the inside of a bowl

convex curved shape like the outside of a bowl

cosmonaut astronaut from the Soviet Union

crater pit or hole made in the surface of a planet or moon by a meteorite crashing into it

disarmament giving up weapons

docking joining together spacecraft in space

electronics use of the flow of electrical charges to make devices such as computers and televisions

escape velocity speed a spacecraft must reach to escape the gravity of a planet and travel away into deep space

friction force that tries to stop one surface from sliding or rolling against another

galaxy group or system of stars. There are billions of galaxies in the universe.

geostationary orbit placement of a satellite in space at such a height and speed that it stays in position above the same point on Earth's surface

gravity force that pulls a smaller body towards a larger body

gunpowder explosive powder made by mixing charcoal, sulfur, and potassium nitrate

gyroscope spinning device for keeping balance. Gyroscopes are fitted in navigation systems for aircraft, missiles, and spacecraft.

ham radio amateur radio that is usually operated from the home

integrated circuit electronic device made up of thousands of miniature parts wired together on a slice of silicon material, known as a chip

laser device that produces a narrow but very strong beam of light

lens curved piece of glass or other transparent material that lets light through it, either bringing together or spreading the rays

light year measurement of space based on the distance light can travel in one year

missile anything thrown or fired, such as a stone, arrow, or bullet

module part of a larger piece of equipment or system

National Aeronautics and Space Administration (NASA) government organization set up in 1958 to run the U.S. space program

nuclear weapon bomb with enormous destructive power obtained by changing matter into energy

orbit path followed by a satellite around a larger body

oxygen gas found in air, essential to human life

payload amount of weight that a rocket can lift into orbit or send on a spaceflight

radar system for tracking objects or measuring how fast they are traveling. It uses radio beams that bounce off an object and travel back to a receiver.

radiation energy given off in the form of light, electricity, or heat

reflection bouncing back of light rays or sound waves as they hit a surface

refraction bending of light rays as they pass from one substance to another, for instance, from air to water

rehydrate to add water to a substance (such as dried food) to bring it back to its original form

robot machine that carries out tasks it has been taught or that can be controlled by a computer or a person

rotation turning or spinning motion, moving in a circle like a wheel

satellite something that orbits a larger body, such as a moon orbiting a planet

soft landing controlled descent onto a moon or planet, using rockets, parachutes, or air bags

solar system Sun and the nine planets, including Earth, that orbit it

Soviet Union federation of communist republics led by Russia, which broke up in 1991

spectroscope special telescope for studying the spectrum of light from stars

step rocket rocket in two or three sections. Each section has its own engines and falls off when its fuel is used up.

sunspot cooler, dark patch on the surface of the sun

supersonic traveling faster than the speed of sound

synthetic artifically made

More Books to Read

Casanellas, Antonio. *Great Discoveries & Inventions*. Milwaukee: Gareth Stevens Inc., 2000.

Erlbach, Arlene. *The Kids' Invention Book*. Minneapolis: The Lerner Publishing Group, 1998.

Tesar, Jenny E., and Bryan H. Bunch. *The Blackbirch Encyclopedia of Science & Invention*. Woodbridge, Conn.: Blackbirch Press, 2001.

Index

Apollo spacecraft 23, 24, 27, 29, 35
astronomers 8, 10, 13

black holes 43

Challenger 39
Cold War 20
Copernicus, Nicolaus 8

docking missions 23

electronics 5, 16, 21, 28
escape velocity 16
extra-vehicular activity (EVA) 40–41

food and drink 32–33, 35
friction 17, 38

Gagarin, Yuri 22, 23, 24 25, 32
galaxies 5, 13, 43
Galileo 8, 9, 42
geostationary orbit 18, 19
Gilruth, Robert 23
Glenn, John 23
Global Positioning System (GPS) 21
Goddard, Robert H. 10, 11
gravity 4, 10, 14, 16, 31, 33, 40
gyroscopes 17

health in space 33, 35
Herschel, William 9
Hubble, Edwin 43
Hubble Space Telescope 9, 21, 42–43

International Space Station 5, 35, 39

Jansky, Karl 12
jet packs 40, 41
Jodrell Bank 13
Jupiter 8, 17

Manned Maneuvering Unit (MMU) 41
manned spacecraft 22–23, 29, 30, 31, 34–35, 38–39
Mars 31, 36–37
Mir space station 33, 34, 35
missiles 10, 15, 20, 23, 26
Moon 8, 17, 26, 27, 28, 29, 30, 31

NASA 15, 17, 21, 23, 25, 27, 28, 31, 35, 36, 39, 41
Newton, Sir Isaac 7, 9, 14

Oberth, Hermann 10, 11, 14
orbit 4, 8, 14, 16, 18, 20, 34, 36, 38, 42
oxygen 10, 25, 26, 30, 37, 38

radar 5, 17, 20
radiation 12, 17, 25
Reber, Grote 13
Ride, Sally 39
robot explorers 30, 31, 36, 37
rockets 5, 6–7, 10–11, 14, 16, 20, 26, 27, 38

satellites 5, 14, 15, 18–19, 20–21, 42
Saturn 5 rocket 26, 27, 28
Skylab 27, 34–35
solar system 5, 17, 36
space probes 16–17, 31, 36, 37
space race 5, 16, 20, 28
space shuttles 23, 25, 38–39, 42, 43
space sickness 33, 35
space stations 25, 34–35
space walks 24, 25, 40–41
spectroscopes 17
Sputnik 14, 15, 22
sunspots 8

telescopes 4, 5, 8–9, 12–13, 42–43
Tsiolkovski, Konstantin 10, 11

Van Allen, James 15
Von Braun, Wernher 26, 27